About the Book

The last frontier on earth for enterprising and adventurous people is the sea. In this absorbing book the noted science writer, Erik Bergaust, looks ahead to the near future, when we will build offshore cities. Employing fascinating new information, Bergaust shows how today, at last, we have the scientific and technological know-how to meet the challenge of the sea. And today we have the incentive because of our growing need for food, fresh water, minerals, power, and weather control. What will life be like in the sea cities? In his penetrating look into the future Bergaust shows how a career in oceanography can be interesting and worthwhile for young people.

Colonizing the Sea

ERIK BERGAUST

G. P. Putnam's Sons · New York

Library of Congress Cataloging in Publication Data
Bergaust, Erik
Colonizing the Sea
Includes index.
Summary: Discusses the possibility of sea
cities as man employs his latest technological
knowledge to use this last frontier to his best
advantage.
1. Oceanography—Juvenile literature. 2. Mari-
culture—Juvenile literature. 3. Ocean engineering
—Juvenile literature. [1. Oceanography.
2. Ocean engineering] I. Title.
GC21.5.B47 1976   620'.416'2   76-21355

Contents

ACKNOWLEDGMENTS

Close cooperation by many official and semi-official sources made it possible to write this book. They include the Department of the Navy, the Department of Interior, U.S. Naval School for Deep Sea Divers, the U.S. Senate Committee on Commerce, the Energy Research & Development Administration, the American Gas Association, and the Scripps Institution of Oceanography.

The author also appreciates the assistance rendered by many individuals and corporations. Incalculable cooperation was provided by the U.S. Steel Corporation and the American Petroleum Institute. The latter organization gave permission to use material from Dr. Athelstan Spilhaus' article in its magazine "Petroleum Today." Thanks also to Paul J. Saxton of the United States Information Agency for much assistance.

Some of the material is based on information provided in the books *The Sea* (Life Nature Library); *Ships That Explore the Deep* and *Skin Divers in Action* (both G. P. Putnam's Sons). Some information was reprinted with permission of the American Gas Association (catalog on the "Atlantic Action Program"). Most of the illustrations were provided by the U.S. Navy unless otherwise stated.

ERIK BERGAUST
Washington, D. C.

Colonizing the Sea

1

The Last Frontier

A new frontier is opening to mankind in the closing decades of the twentieth century. It is the last frontier on earth for enterprising and adventurous people. It is life in the sea.

Oceans cover 70.8 percent of the earth's surface. The total amount of water in the oceans of earth dazes the mind: *330 million cubic miles.* Compared to this vastness, the volume of all land above sea level is only one eighteenth as large. Even the largest landmass, Eurasia, shrinks to island size when we match it to the great widths and depths of the sea.

All humans are basically islanders, and we have treated the great waters of earth as little more than hunting grounds for fishermen and highways for ships. We pride ourselves on the sophisticated ways we have learned to cope with life on land, and yet we remain primitive about the sea.

Centuries ago people learned it was foolish to hunt wild animals for all the meat they wanted. They tamed, raised, and slaughtered animals —cattle, sheep, and hogs—in order to meet their needs. It is possible for people to do the same with fish. Yet today we still hunt the seas for fish in the primitive way our ancestors once hunted the woods and grasslands for animals. In our hunting for fish we take about 60 million tons a year from the seas. If we would *raise* fish, as we do cattle, we could harvest many times 60 million tons at a time when two thirds of the four

11

billion people on earth are hungry, many of them literally starving to death.

But there are many more things in the sea than fish. Sooner or later everything on earth is carried into the oceans through the weather cycle, water runoffs, and erosion. Water can dissolve more substances than any other liquid known. It has an unusually high capacity for storing heat. In a variety of ways the properties of water make our planet hospitable to life. For example, other liquids contract when they solidify, but water expands by nine percent when it freezes. This means ice floats instead of sinking. Thus ice is accessible to the sun's rays, which limit its spreading and the depths of cold polar seas remain unfrozen, allowing some forms of life to survive there.

The sea is, of course, salty. Its average salinity is 3.5 percent, which means that a cubic mile of sea water contains 166 million tons of salt. It comes from the breaking up of rocks and the wearing away of mountains. Altogether the seas of the world contain enough salt to cover the earth's land surface with a layer 500 feet thick.

Other prominent elements in the sea besides salt are magnesium, calcium, potassium, and bromine. There is abundant magnesium in the oceans, and it is well worth harvesting. In the sea you'll find zinc, iron, aluminum, lead, tin, nickel, silver, mercury, and traces of all the other metals. There is even gold in the sea, though not enough to make it worthwhile to prospect for—38 pounds per cubic mile of sea water.

Of course the sea has always been there, challenging humans. But not until recently, as we use up our resources on land, have we begun to realize what potential waits there. Beneath the waves lies a vast virgin territory every bit as challenging as outer space and infinitely more promising of economic reward.

Today, at last, we have the scientific and technological know-how to meet the challenge of the sea. And today we have the incentive to conquer the sea because of our growing need for food, fresh water, minerals, power, and weather control. Still a third reason for the drive toward the new frontier of the sea is our great desire to preserve all that we can of our land environment against the onslaught of many kinds of pollution.

Mankind's last frontier lies in the oceans and their floors. This view of the ocean floor was taken by the research vessel Trieste. *In future sea farms starfish such as these will be weeded out so that sea farmers can cultivate fish, lobsters, and other food sources. (U.S. Navy)*

The sea is not as mysterious as it was in the time of the ancients, when great thinkers like Plato and Aristotle speculated over its nature. Now we know that high and low tides are caused by the gravitational pull of the moon and the sun, which act like magnets. Indeed, we know all sorts of things that puzzled the ancients. For example, we know:

• Tides have a great affect on marine life. Marine organisms and plants are carried toward the shores at high tides. Fish of all sizes follow this flow of food since it is easier for them to feed in shallow waters. As the tide goes out, millions of organisms are left along the beaches as food for birds, or the organisms die and become fertilizer for shore-line areas.

• The rotation of the earth causes currents in the oceans. Forces derived from the earth's spin and location in space are basic to all movement of water on the earth's surface. The force of winds, also set in motion by the earth's rotation, contributes to the flow of currents. Intensity and speed of currents are influenced, too, by ocean depth, temperature, and even the degree of salt in the water.

Knowledge of such facts has grown over the centuries as a result of fascinating studies by a great variety of people doing all sorts of interesting things. Their work, called oceanography, or sometimes referred to as ocean science, is the common name for a whole array of scientific disciplines pertaining to the sea. It is no wonder that so many young people these days are finding careers in oceanography. Each of the scientific disciplines in oceanography usually has a specific name. For example, *submarine geology* is the science dealing with the topography of the sea bottom, what developed it, and the nature of sedimentation. Another area, *marine biology,* treats the living organisms in the oceans and the chemical and physical nature of their environment. All told, oceanography involves several hundred scientific disciplines.

But more than just oceanographers will be needed in this development of the earth's last frontier—the colonizing of the sea. It will require both men and women—engineers, planners, teachers, divers, agriculturalists, mechanics, doctors, lawyers and technicians of every conceivable kind. And poets and historians will be welcome in the effort, too.

14

Indeed, everything that people do on land will have to be done in the cities of the future on the surface of the sea—and, possibly at some later date, in the cities which are created *under* the sea. And the creators of these future communities will have to display greater imagination and skill than their ancestors showed in the huge land cities of civilization.

2

Pioneers of the Last Frontier

People are running out of living space. In order to give us the things we need to live comfortably and at the same time to preserve a clean environment, it takes increasing effort on the part of everyone. The sort of living standards we seek, coupled with the exploding population growth, require higher food outputs, increased industrial production, more utilities for heat, light, air conditioning, sewage plants, and other facilities. As metropolitan areas grow, they constantly require more service facilities. To cope with this situation we must stop cluttering our land with sewage plants, power-generating stations, factories, oil refineries, storage tanks, and airports.

The sea offers people extraordinary space close to the crowded coasts, the majority of the world's cities, and the principal terminals of trade. So far man has broadened his use of the coastline by extending it inland. He has not extended it out to sea much. In the future land use plans must also involve plans for sea use. An imaginative, adventurous ocean utilization program could multiply our living space. It is not quite true that "They don't make land anymore." We *can* make more "land" by expanding into the sea with structures and facilities that will constitute "service cities" for the "mother cities" on the mainland.

In recent years there have been many pioneers of that new frontier—cities in the sea. They include such people as the crews of nuclear submarines and of lonely weather ships in the icy North Atlantic, and scientists manning research stations on ice islands drifting through the Arctic. All lead cramped lives at sea, far from the so-called comfort of so-called civilization, yet all perform useful work and survive quite cheerfully far from land.

Among these pioneers of a future way of life are the people—both men and women—who operate and live on oil-drilling equipment and rigs many miles from land. These huge structures of concrete and steel are man-made islands anchored to the ocean floor and left to withstand the hazards of gales and hurricanes. Their link to the mainland is the radio and the visits of supply ships and helicopters.

Life on an offshore oil or gas platform is tough. Every aspect of the job of raising the oil or gas from the deep is demanding and dangerous Although the modern man-made islands are large, quarters and facilities for their crews are cramped.

Accidents happen on oil-drilling rigs. A gas well may blow out and break into flames and injure people. The escaping gas may burn for days and make rescue by ships and helicopters difficult. But designers and engineers are working hard to improve oil-drilling rigs and make them as safe as possible.

Most offshore oil-drilling rigs are just a few miles from the mainland. But discoveries of oil farther away from the mainland and the introduction of advanced technologies have made it possible to drill for oil far out at sea—in some instances almost 200 miles from land.

For the first oil-drilling operation in the North Sea, between Norway and Great Britain, it was necessary to build an entire artificial island of steel and concrete, float it to the oil field almost 200 miles from Norway, and lower it to rest on the ocean floor more than 200 feet below the surface. Until a pipeline could be constructed, production was dependent upon availability of sea transport interrupted by the North Sea's severe weather conditions.

To overcome the initial problem, it was decided to build a massive concrete island resting on the seabed with storage capacity for up to one million barrels of oil. This unique island, with its huge storage facility,

Rigs such as this mark increased oil drilling activity along our shores. These rigs, where workers live for periods, are like mere log cabins compared to the future cities of the sea. (American Petroleum Institute)

may well be the forerunner for many similar structures to be built throughout the world in the coming decades. The crew manning these islands works two-week shifts and gets two weeks off. At regular intervals they are taken off the island by helicopter and flown to the mainland to join their families and rest.

Offshore oil drilling is by no means restricted to permanent concrete and steel islands or oil-drilling rigs anchored to the ocean floor. All over the world, except in the Antarctic, a considerable amount of oil drilling is done by mobile floating platforms. Today there are scores operating off the United States coast, most of them off Louisiana and Texas. Elsewhere in the world, other countries are also going ahead with marine exploration and drilling from mobile rigs.

These unique "vessels," with ungainly construction, mechanisms, and instrumentation, have been of redeeming value to the oil companies which operate them. They are perhaps the most functional vessels ever built. Engineered for one purpose, they drill efficiently the year round, whatever the weather.

A mobile rig may be about an acre of steel plate supported on a grid of huge metal bottles partly flooded and sunk to a draft of some 40 feet. This leaves the main deck perched some 44 feet above the water surface. The arrangement avoids 70 percent of the force of waves and exposes relatively little bulk to the winds.

The square-shaped mobile rig with its 90-degree lines makes traditional mariners wince. The length of the vessel is some 200 feet, as is the beam. There is no wheel in the wheelhouse for the rig has no rudder. Lacking prow and fantail, the vessel has one side arbitrarily designated the bow, and the opposite side the stern. To the casual eye the vessel is a random clutter of sheds and masts, catwalks and cranes, pipes and chains, motors and controls, communications equipment and monitors.

The serious function of the mobile oil rig begins when the vessel drops its circle of eight anchors weighing twice as much as those of a huge aircraft carrier. Thereafter, unlike conventional ships, the less the rig travels, the more successful the voyage. The destination of the vessel is "straight down," say, in 849 feet of water in the Santa Barbara

One of the new breed of sea pioneering equipment in the Deep Sea Drilling Project's drilling research vessel Glomar Challenger. *She conducts drilling operations in the open ocean, using a new technique to maintain position over a hole. (Scripps Institution of Oceanography)*

Channel some nine miles off the coast of California. To drill at this water depth the vessel must have stability, and that is really the name of the vessel's game. In a sea with ten-foot waves the rig will heave less than one foot. It is not unusual for the rigs to cope with winds of more than 100 knots and waves as high as 30 feet.

The mobile rigs perform a good amount of exploration—the second step in developing a marine oil field. Geologic and seismic studies come first to see if a likely oil-bearing sedimentary structure exists beneath the ocean floor. Then mobile rigs move in to drill into the structure, hoping to find oil. Sometimes they do. More often drilling yields only scientific information on the rocks below the sea floor. But when the mobile rig does establish the existence of an oil field, stationary platforms will be built, each with the capacity for drilling many wells—sometimes 20 or 30—fanning out into the structure below. Systems are being designed now which may make the fixed platform unnecessary. Remotely controlled oil production equipment would be fixed on the sea floor and pipelines would carry oil to a central man-made island with storage and docking facilities for tankers.

While drilling, a drift by the mobile rig could mean trouble for the string of large-diameter pipe hanging beneath the platform. Called the "riser," this string of pipe serves as an umbilical cord between the rig and the hole being drilled into the sea floor. Through the riser a smaller drill pipe is guided into the hole. The skipper trims his ship by pumping water ballast to and from the submerged flotation members. The position is maintained by adjusting tension on the wrist-thick anchor cables. Providing muscle are four gigantic winches encased in the ship's four corners.

In his maneuvers the skipper is assisted by some instruments of noble simplicity and some of far-out sophistication. Levels of mercury in glass tubes resemble glorified carpenter's levels and work much the same way. Finally, the skipper uses an electronic sonar computer whose display screen indicates whether the rig is holding steady, usually a mere eight feet off the dead center of the well. That is less than one percent of the rig's depth—and very good and absolutely safe. The riser has the

Every year increasing thousands of Americans engage in underwater activity. Here an aquanaut trainee struggles with a lighting system outside a Navy habitat. His job is like that of an astronaut when working outside his space ship. (U.S. Navy)

elasticity to handle a drift of ten percent. Most rigs seldom exceed two percent.

The operation calls for oft-repeated withdrawal and reinsertion of the drill string. For two action-filled hours the 90-foot lengths of pipe are hoisted out of the hole. Huge tongs are used to unscrew the stands of pipe. Floor crewmen coordinate their movements like defensive football linemen. The driller manipulates the draw work with a fine touch. The derrick man wrestles the extracted pipes into a neat stack. It takes ten minutes to change bits; then two more hours to put it all back together again.

As with any engineering creation, the proof is in the performance. It is considered good if a mobile rig can complete five wells per year when operating in water as deep as 1,200 feet. One U.S. mobile rig, the Blue Water II, has drilled 40 wells over a seven-year span (370,000 feet of hole, or 70 miles into the earth). This performance is significant for the future, at a time of increasing energy demands.

Offshore drilling has created one of those arguments that probably never can be resolved to everyone's satisfaction. Strict environmentalists want no offshore drilling at all. But the oil companies, citing the critical and increasing need of fuel, claim a good safety record in drilling with few spills that pose serious pollution threats.

3

Offshore Service Cities

Comparing the oil rig of today with the future city in the sea visualized by planners is like comparing a log cabin to a high-rise apartment house. The planners speak with persuasive logic when discussing what they visualize for the future.

Service facilities for a modern city, including docks, railroad yards, airports, power-generating stations, sewage plants, and various factories and plants, usually require hundreds, or even thousands, of acres of land. The price of this land has skyrocketed to such proportions that the high costs of operating the facilities, resulting in heavy taxation of citizens, have reached prohibitive levels.

Another growing problem for the big cities is pollution. A city's service facilities are usually smelly, noisy, dirty, and ugly. Sometimes these facilities are potential fire hazards. And a maze of factory chimneys, oil refinery stacks, and power station grids is always ugly.

Harbors traditionally are a difficult point where traffic, tides, winds, and shoals often combine to turn a safe refuge into a potentially hazardous place. Paradoxically, as ships grow larger, some of them cannot even enter certain harbors.

Refineries are being banned from the coastlines of Delaware, Maine, New Jersey, Florida, and other coastal states. Even when refineries are not banned, environmental restrictions make it economically impossible for industry to go ahead with the urgent plan to supply the energy we need. So the challenge of supplying this energy beckons us to the sea.

Within the next few years the United States will need dozens of new refineries, each costing about $150 million and requiring three years to build. But environmental restrictions are preventing their construction.

The way to contain the pollution associated with these refineries is to use the sea imaginatively. People live on the coastline, and, obviously, power plants must be near people. That's why it is logical to build power plants off the coast, where the huge amounts of water required for their cooling are readily accessible and where the plants cannot harm a heavily populated environment.

The cheapest ways of transporting oil are by tanker over the sea and by pipeline overland. The larger the tanker, the more economical it is. And the safer it is, the fewer oil spills there will be. Yet no harbors in the United States can handle the new half-million-ton tankers. By off-loading these tankers into small barges, the risk of spills and pollution increases. So why not take the harbor out to sea? In the future superports for supertankers should become part of great city-in-the-sea complexes.

Nuclear power plants have caused considerable concern to environmentalists. Because of radiation hazards, such facilities require vast areas of surrounding land for protection. Also, they require tremendous amounts of water for cooling. Certainly such power plants may be constructed in the sea to great advantage. (And, as we shall see later, they can be built on floating rigs and located so far from the shoreline that people won't even be able to spot them on the horizon.)

Effects of the thermal discharge—the water which becomes heated in its cooling process—can be accommodated more easily in an offshore plant. Discharge water will dissipate its heat into a small area of the ocean. It has been estimated that the discharge from a two-unit offshore installation will result in an average temperature increase of only five degrees for a surface area of approximately five acres. In addition,

Artist's concept of undersea vehicle—submersible—which would be used for mining ore on the ocean floor and bringing other treasures of the deep to our civilization in coming decades. (U.S. Steel)

the circulating water discharge system can be specifically designed to take into account the local ecological situation and potentially enhance conditions for sea farming.

Fishing as an industry for American vessels has only one hope if it is to prosper in the future. It must take a technological leap into automation. In order to justify the cost, fishing vessels must spend more time at sea and less in port. They should use fish factories and processing plants in a complex out at sea, separating the seafood wastes from the food parts and sending the food to shore through pipelines.

Organic wastes from the factories and wastes from the land could be treated and piped to undersea portions of the complexes for use as nutrients in fish farming. Thus aquaculture would grow around the city just as agriculture surrounds our land cities.

Likewise, city sewage plants may be located offshore and the treated waste materials made into useful products for a city in the sea or for other locations. Sewage plants require large areas, as do many other service facilities. They, too, belong off the shoreline.

Desalination plants are being constructed throughout the world to cope with the increasing shortage of fresh water. Such facilities require acres of land for economical operation. It is logical that such plants must be *near* the sea. But it is even more logical that they be constructed *in* the sea.

One fascinating aspect of the use of sea space is how city planners and architects propose building big airports off the shoreline within the next few years. In order to cope with increased air traffic, the United States will need almost seven hundred new airports over the next ten years. Of that number six hundred would serve private and business aircraft. Yet more than forty major new airports for increasingly bigger airliners will be needed for such cities as New York, St. Louis, Atlanta, Boston, Honolulu, Minneapolis, and Louisville. This program will cost billions of dollars and will require literally thousands of acres of land. Every one of these valuable acres for runways, parking facilities,

28

Powered by pressurized gas stored in steel seamless pressure vessels, this sleek undersea vehicle could play a prominent role in mining precious ores economically and preserving fish and plant life near offshore service cities. (U.S. Steel)

hangars, terminals, and roads will be covered by concrete. Yet we must consider the possibility of building as many of them as possible in the sea. Of course, this concept cannot apply to cities such as Louisville or St. Louis, but it certainly applies to many other large cities.

City planners and architects, when designing airports for the future, must take into consideration the amount of traffic and the kinds of airplanes that will prevail many decades from now. Any large city airport on the drawing board today is geared to cope with the traffic situation which will materialize around the year 2000.

Visualize a 20,000-foot runway for aircraft jutting out into the ocean from some central point a few miles from the shoreline. It will resemble a long, straight bridge. Indeed, it will be built like a modern bridge—out of strong steel beams and girders anchored to the ocean bottom. And it will even serve as a bridge. While the top surface of the structure constitutes a long runway for planes, the space underneath may be taken up by docks for fishing vessels, a monorail transportation system for airline passengers and a highway for cars. Underneath the surface of the water and all the way to the bottom space is available for other facilities—submerged storage facilities, pipelines for fresh water from adjacent desalination plants, pipelines for fish from factories built at the very end of the runway, cables for carrying electric power from nearby generating plants.

In the steel structure underneath the runway it will also be possible to construct city sewage facilities. Sewage may be irradiated with electron beams to destroy viruses and bacteria. Sewage could then be returned to the land or the ocean as a fertilizer, rather than as a pollutant. Low-grade heat from various parts of the city-in-the-sea complex (so-called "waste heat"), discharged from different power plants, may be used also in aquaculture to regulate the temperature of the water to the optimum conditions for fish farming.

Among the steel pilings a miraculous aquatic life will begin to flourish and become part of the aquaculture operations. In addition to algae and plankton, clusters of living, growing organisms will soften the angular lines of the steel reef beams and girders—barnacles, flowerlike

A capsule and free-swimming divers will be used to investigate the sea floor in the construction of a great sea city. This is an artist's concept of the Naval Civil Engineering Laboratory's Naval Experimental Manned Observatory (NEMO) system as it will appear when manned at a 600-foot depth on the sea floor. (U.S. Navy)

sea anemones feeding with tentacles outstretched, moss animals, feathery sea worms extending from tubes they build out of calcium carbonate, delicate gorgonians, or sea fans, spiny sea urchins, and even precious black coral.

Up above, jet planes take off and land. Underneath, fast monorail trains shoot back and forth on two or three different tracks or levels. Further down we find pipelines and cables. What started out as a straight structure for a runway jutting out into the sea some 20,000 feet has become a supercomplex and a conglomerate of service facilities. Needless to say, this concept is economical since so many users (and customers) will share the cost.

From this point we may speculate on how additional runways and structures and modules may be put together to form a network containing the complete facilities for operating a modern airport. Use of the extra space underneath the surface structures for service facilities, ranging from lighthouses and weather stations to marinas for pleasure boats and fishing vessels, will create a unique underwater city complex with many purposes.

Minerals, such as mined phosphate rock or magnesium, could be extracted from the sea at such complex sites. One of the great costs of extracting things from seawater is the need to pump huge amounts of water. The same pumps and the same water could be used for several purposes—extracting minerals, producing fresh water, cooling power plants, and air conditioning.

In discussing the prospects of cities in the sea, Dr. Athelstan Spilhaus, one of the nation's leading scientists and an active participant in many of the nation's advanced science programs, points out some interesting aspects:

"A city anywhere must start with a purpose. Then people come to work, homes are built for the workers, and thus the city grows. The multiple uses constitute the real purpose of a sea city. With airports and harbors travelers will need hotels. Hotels at airports on land have to be insulated from aircraft noise. What better insulator could there

be than sea water? Hotel accommodations could be built within the huge floats or pylons beneath the sea surface. Travelers would truly have an 'ocean view'—from below!

"Airports are in the same plight as power plants. They need to be near people. Yet they occupy huge tracts of land near cities that people need for other purposes. Traffic congestion on the ground to and from the center of the city reduces the airport's usefulness. Airports are under fire for aircraft noise, and in some places planes are restricted in use of power on takeoffs and landings, which either increases the hazard of flying or increases the cost of the aircraft. Couldn't airports join the complex at sea?"

How can we, in the United States, carve out the whole system for cities in the sea in a planned way instead of whittling at it piecemeal?

Dr. Spilhaus suggests that it is probably not economical for an individual activity (for example, oil refining) to move out to sea as a single activity and be able in the short time scale available to meet our urgent demands for energy. But if we join uses in a systems concept with a common kind of underpinning, moving out to sea would be feasible, he believes.

"First of all," he says, "we need public policy that will recognize that the dimensions of the task are very large indeed. The government's initiative and commitment must be comparable to national goals that we have achieved in space and atomic energy. The Maritime Administration with its harbor problems, the Energy Research and Development Administration (ERDA) with its nuclear plants, the Environmental Protection Agency (EPA) with its waste disposal program, and the National Oceanic and Atmospheric Administration (NOAA) with its experimental platforms might join with the Federal Aviation Administration (FAA) and its airports to plan a synergistic sea system. Such discussions are already taking place. I wonder, however, whether inter-agency cooperation is sufficient. We will need to jump the barrier that defines traditional missions of government departments."

Thus the U.S. should perhaps esablish a new and independent agency or "administration" for the development of the sea cities. The

Similar to a Skylab space station, this habitat design shows how the experts plan to build sea floor dwellings of tomorrow. This Tektite station is the prototype of habitats that will be commonplace in future decades. (U.S. Navy)

government has done this before by establishing the Atomic Energy Commission (now ERDA) for nuclear power development and the National Aeronautics and Space Administration (NASA) for space flight. Perhaps we could draw from a number of existing government agencies representing the many different aspects of the sea complexes to establish a new department.

If we move complexes out to sea, we become involved with problems of international maritime law. Practical considerations in building are dictated by nature—such as, how steeply does the sea bottom shelve into deep water? These considerations may conflict with arbitrary coastal limits of three, twelve, fifty, or more miles. Where water is shallow, as in the Gulf of Mexico, it will be necessary to go far out; where water is deeper, not as far. But these legal problems can be solved.

Eventually the complexity of a sea city could become immense. In the beginning the sea complexes will be designed to serve as service facilities for their "mother cities." But many experts visualize that sometime in the future the cities in the sea will include schools, shops, homes for people working at the facilities, and an array of the more conventional things we find in the cities on the mainland, perhaps even a small park or garden spot with lawns and trees.

Do we have the technology at hand to build such structures? The answer is a qualified yes. Experts say it is simpler to draw up plans for such cities today than it was for our space agency to plan the Apollo trips to the moon back in the sixties.

Our experience from marine construction, the building of superships, submarines, deep-diving equipment, ocean cables, and enormous steel structures such as bridges and skyscrapers, makes it possible for today's engineers to plan a city in the sea much as they would plan a modern city somewhere on the mainland.

The effort of building a city in the sea is probably larger than even the largest of our industries could undertake alone. In industry there will have to be associations of our very largest industrial concerns to achieve the building of a complex. Far from discouraging partnerships among the largest industries, we will need to encourage new kinds of combinations, new kinds of consortiums of industries, perhaps in the manner of the space program. Designers and engineers interested in the city-in-the-sea concept agree that we have advanced far enough to master the technology required. The steel industry of the United States, in particular, has vast experience in building all the structures needed for the various segments of a city in the sea.

American Bridge Division of U.S. Steel, for example, has built an 1,800-foot pipeline installation for the Van Norman Reservoir in California. About 680 tons of plate were fabricated into 52 sections of 10-foot diameter steel pipe. A more complicated piece of plumbing was a 217-ton T-section of steel pipe fabricated by the same company. The giant pipe, 23 feet in diameter, was first assembled at the factory in San Francisco, then disassembled into 56 shipping pieces to travel by rail and truck to the New Melones Dam and Reservoir project on the Stanislaus River. There it was reassembled in an underground water diversion tunnel. The diversion tunnel liner was formed in part by a series of 23-foot diameter, 80-foot-long sections of welded steel pipe, each weighing approximately 170 tons.

American tank and pressure vessel manufacturers have built 7.5-million-gallon water tanks and have fabricated storage tanks for petroleum products, liquid gases, and all kinds of chemicals. Some of the pressure vessels fabricated at American Bridge Division's Orange, Texas, plants are 300 feet in length and weigh up to 500 tons each. One of the more unusual steel plate projects to come out of the company's Orange plant was the fabrication of 37 double-skinned tunnel sections approximately 300 feet in length. The long "cans" were towed from Orange, Texas, to Chesapeake Bay, where they were used to form part of the Chesapeake Bay Bridge-Tunnel.

Barges made of steel, and measuring 50 feet by 240 feet and weighing 450 tons, have been built by the thousands in the United States. Immensely strong steel structures, plate-weldment girders, and other support items for bridges, tunnels, and skyscrapers are manufactured on a routine basis by the American steel companies. Many experts say that the actual construction of a sea city represents the least of the

Some day it will be feasible to haul oil and liquefied gas by submarine tankers. The gigantic submarines will offload at tank farms and underwater pipeline stations which are a part of the future cities in the sea. Here an artist conceives how special diver crews will handle the tricky part of the operation. (American Petroleum Institute)

problems involved in the building of such a city. It is, they say, the complexity of the systems approach of putting many different functions together, as in a puzzle—and the management of it—that represents the true challenge. It is, in fact, the uniqueness of the concept that makes it such a tremendous job.

4

Resources Beneath the Waves

The sea shapes the world's surface, moderates its climate, and cradles its life. Locked up in the sea is a great variety of salts, minerals, and organic matter in solution. Oxygen, carbon dioxide, and nitrogen from the atmosphere are also dissolved in sea water. The oxygen is what marine creatures breathe; the carbon dioxide is used by green plants in the sea to produce food.

A cubic mile of sea water contains 166 million tons of salt. In addition to salt, the ocean is an important source of magnesium metal, bromine, and a number of other substances widely used in industry. Portions of the salt have come from the breaking up of rocks by frost and erosion and the gradual wearing away of mountains, which releases locked-in chemicals and permits them to be carried down to the ocean by rain water. Additional salt has come from rocks beneath the ocean bed. The process has been going on for millions of years.

Salts washed into the sea constitute only a small portion of all the material that is constantly being carried into it from land areas. Debris from the grinding down of forests, mountains, and fields, as well as dust, volcanic ash, and meteorite particles from outer space settle on the ocean floor. Mixed in with the debris from above the surface are the remains of marine organisms in the ocean itself. As these organisms die, they drift downward. However, many of them do not reach the ocean

A "Deep Quest" research vehicle beneath the surface of the Pacific Ocean before descending 8,310 feet. (U.S. Navy)

floor, but are consumed on the way down by deeper-dwelling organisms.

In relatively shallow waters, where marine life is richest, and near the mouths of rivers which bring down debris from the land, the accumulations of debris are thousands of feet thick. These sediments represent a great potential for a variety of resources. Shallow waters close to the shorelines are of particular interest to those contemplating construction of cities in the sea. It is in these waters that we harvest seafood, drill for oil, and search for minerals and other resources.

These areas of coastal waters, called continental shelves, are shallow platforms adjacent to the continents or some large islands. They stretch outward from the shore until a marked increase in the slope of the ocean floor begins. Their most important feature—shallowness—controls somewhat the swell which rolls in from deeper parts of the ocean and makes the establishment of man-made structures along its edge feasible. Most of the fish in the oceans are found in the waters of the continental shelves.

Naturally these continental shelves have been more thoroughly explored and surveyed than the remainder of the ocean floor because of their importance to mariners who use soundings and bottom samples as aids to navigation. Surveying these waters is an endless task because earthquake activity underneath the ocean floor frequently changes the bottom contours considerably.

In recent years the shelf has gained added importance because of the large amount of minerals found on and beneath its floor. In 1946 the United States took possession of the mineral rights on the continental shelf adjacent to its shores, the 100-fathom curve being defined as its outer limit. In many other parts of the world, however, the outer limit of the shelf, where a marked increase in slope is noted, lies at a different depth. The average shelf in the world has a width of about 42 miles, and it has been estimated that the shelves cover about 7.6 percent of the earth's surface.

The shelf was once believed to be a gentle, continuously sloping plain, but now we know this is true only in specific locations. Often the shelf is hilly and has many irregularities. Examples of shelves with

41

rough bottoms are found adjacent to landmasses which were once covered by glaciers. Deep depressions, such as the fjords in Norway and British Columbia, or deep troughs, such as the Gulf of Saint Lawrence and the Strait of Juan de Fuca, penetrate far into the land and often extend across the shelves, but with shallower depths seaward.

Those steep bays frequently have many basins containing muddy sediments combined with gravel and sand. Many banks rising close to sea level, including the Grand Banks of Newfoundland and Georges Bank off New England, extend along the outer shelf and are covered by sand and gravel. They furnish the best fishing grounds in the world. Numerous hills, mostly mantled with rock or covered with boulders or gravel, are sometimes located on the inner shelf.

Shelves with a smoother bottom are those with elongated sandbanks and depressions. This bottom relief is found on the shelf adjoining the shore of New Jersey and resembles the topography on land. These shelves are mostly covered with sand or a combination of mud and sand. In areas subject to severe storms or strong tidal currents, such as the North Sea or the area off Nantucket, elongated banks are shifting constantly and have to be sounded frequently to warn the mariner of changing conditions. A narrow shelf subjected to strong currents is found on the east coast of Florida and also off Cape Hatteras.

On the Pacific coast the shelves located off young mountain ranges are mostly narrow and deeper than the average, or they are absent entirely. An interesting example of a missing shelf is found on the west coast of South America, where the land declines in a five-degree slope from the crest of the Andes Mountains to the bottom of a trench offshore.

The Atlantic Continental Shelf, of course, is of particular interest to the United States, and fortunately enough, it appears to be among the most promising in the world, as far as resources are concerned. Drilling for oil and gas and the search for minerals may be undertaken in many places along this shelf. Last but not least, it lends itself to construction of cities in the sea at many places, as well as to construction of superports for supertankers, offshore nuclear power plants, and airports.

Computer-controlled robot manipulators such as this are being prepared to perform sensitive, hazardous work in developing resources beneath the sea. To show what intricate tasks it can perform, this manipulator is using a putty knife to remove the top from a paint can—without spilling a drop. (U.S. Navy)

"Rich as the ooze and bottom of the sea with sumless treasures," Shakespeare wrote in *King Henry IV, Part 2*. If he had possessed our present-day knowledge of undersea life, Shakespeare might have been referring to the bottom of the continental shelves. Our knowledge of geology suggests the importance of exploring the Atlantic shelf for gas and oil reserves. Gas and oil are thought to result from the decay and decomposition of plant and animal life which has been buried in the earth. Since concentrations of these organic materials are required and burial must occur, it is entirely reasonable to expect petroleum deposits to be located at places where rivers and glaciers have dumped their loads of soil, rock, and organic debris in the distant past.

Added to the organic matter coming from onshore areas are the remains of aquatic plants and animals that live and die in and around slowly deposited sea-bottom sediments. Through hundreds of millions of years great masses have slowly and continually been washed and scraped into the Atlantic, forming the outer continental shelf.

Atlantic shelf deposits vary widely in thickness, reaching more than 15,000 feet deep in some areas. At their thickest points these sediments are almost as deep as the highest North American mountains stand above sea level. As different portions of the landmasses are swept into the sea, the sediments change character. Organic material slowly becomes buried deep enough to be subjected to the great pressures of overlying sediment, as well as to the higher temperatures of the earth's interior. Scientists believe that the heat and pressure aid in the conversion of decayed plant and animal matter into hydrocarbons—gas and oil. The same heat and pressure facilitate the transformation of the enclosing sediments into rock of various types.

The outer continental shelf of the Atlantic off the east coast of the U.S. covers an area approximately 162,000 square miles, about equivalent to the area of all the New England states, New York, Pennsylvania, and New Jersey. In surface form the Atlantic shelf is a terrace which dips gently seaward. The shelf is defined as extending to a water depth of about 600 feet. However, the actual terrace area is interrupted by the more steeply inclined continental slope at water depths varying from 150 to 500 feet.

The continental slope extends outward and downward to a median depth of about 6,500 feet. It appears as a narrow band paralleling the outer edge of the shelf in the north and widens to form a plateau in the south. Suitable sedimentary deposits for gas and oil formation are found both on the shelf and the slope. The most attractive areas, where very thick sediments have accumulated, are located from 30 to 300 miles from the shore at the outer portions of the shelf or on the continental slope just beyond the shelf.

Exploratory work to find hydrocarbons begins with seismic surveying. Offshore seismic searches are conducted by creating sharp sound wave pulses in the water which travel through the water and deep into the rock formations below. By measuring reflected waves of this seismic energy, instruments aboard a ship are able to provide a geophysicist with data which can be used to determine general configurations of rock strata thousands of feet into the earth. Seismic surveys can indicate structures which might be traps for hydrocarbons. The survey, though, can only indicate subsurface conditions favorable to the generation and accumulation of gas and oil. It cannot *locate* hydrocarbon deposits, the discovery of which requires actual drilling.

The Atlantic offshore area has not yet been tested by drilling exploratory wells. Only indirect exploratory results of seismic surveys and a few shallow core tests have been available for estimating the area's potential. Yet this preliminary work has been so promising that industry is willing to risk hundreds of millions of dollars required for drilling. At the same time conservationists are opposed to any drilling at all.

Three promising areas have been defined on and just beyond the Atlantic shelf. They are thought to have very thick bands of sediments lying in troughs roughly parallel to the shoreline. Southernmost is the Blake Plateau Basin, beginning 150 miles off the northern half of Florida. Farther north, the Baltimore Canyon Basin lies 49 miles off the coastline of Maryland, Delaware, and New Jersey. Still farther north, 70 miles south of Cape Cod and 100 miles southeast of Long Island, is the beginning of the Georges Bank Basin, which extends northeastward toward Nova Scotia off the Canadian coast.

Estimates of potentially recoverable hydrocarbons from the Atlantic offshore vary from 24 to 211 trillion cubic feet of gas and from 2 to 48 billion barrels of oil. Estimates of the total potential which might be available with improved technology range much higher. The true potential cannot be estimated accurately without many years of drilling in the area.

Nearly all of the Canadian Atlantic shelf is presently held under permit or license by industry. Gas and oil have been discovered on the shelf south of Nova Scotia; one well at Sable Island found gas and oil at many different levels. Other promising discoveries nearby have initiated early planning for a pipeline from offshore Nova Scotia to eastern Canadian population centers and New England. This new discovery area could be an extension of the same sedimentary basin which lies 70 miles south of Cape Cod on the Georges Bank.

All of the most promising Atlantic drilling areas are far out of sight of land. Exploratory drilling requires mobile or floating drilling rigs moving to the more promising sites in hundreds of feet of water and boring holes through thousands of feet of rock into the strata considered the most promising for hydrocarbon concentrations. Eventually pipelines could transfer the oil to sea city complexes closer to shore. Superports with storage tanks and refineries for this oil and gas would still be located away from the main coastline.

Before drilling can be done in the U.S. Atlantic waters, leases must be obtained from the federal government through competitive bidding. Offshore lease sales are announced one or more years in advance to allow time for selection of tracts to be leased, estimation of their potential value by both industry and the Interior Department's Bureau of Land Management, and for the preparation of environmental impact statements and the holding of public hearings. It is not an easy job or one that can be undertaken in a hurry.

There are many resources buried beneath the sea besides oil and natural gas. Not long ago the Massachusetts Institute of Technology published a fascinating study by Gustaf Arrhenius of the Scripps Institution of Oceanography which discussed huge deposits of copper and nickel in the depths of the Pacific near the equator.

Scientists from Lamont-Doherty and Scripps Institution of Oceanography deploy a bottom ocean monitor developed by Dr. Robert Gerard. Such a device, measuring water current direction, speed, and suspended particulate matter, would be vital in choosing the site of an offshore city. (Scripps Institution of Oceanography)

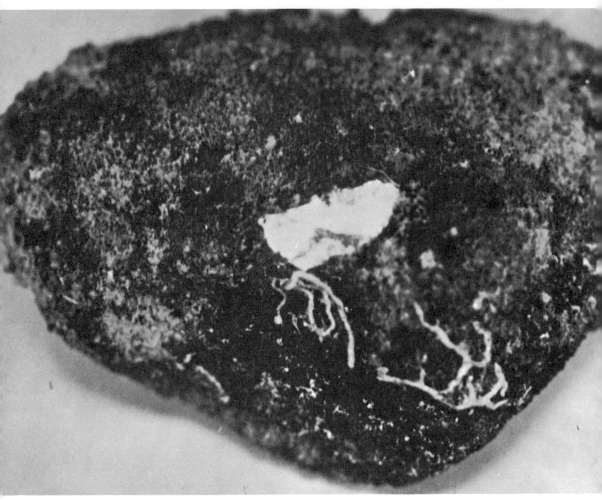

From three miles deep in the equatorial Pacific, this nodule shows the larger bio-genic structures commonly found on surfaces of manganese nodules. The large white spot in the center is a sponge. (Scripps Institution of Oceanography)

"The potential ore body represented by the copper-nickel-rich nodules is immense," wrote Arrhenius. He pointed out that the area north of the equator alone is the size of half that of the United States. "The total mass of copper-nickel-bearing nodules in this and the similar zone south of the equator has been estimated at 10 to 100 billion tons with a content of 10 to 100 million tons of copper and nickel—about the same magnitude as the total estimated resources of copper and nickel on land.

"So, if a major part of just the Pacific deposits proves to be available, this could mean a doubling of the known world resources of these two metals. Whether they can be made available depends on complex geological, technological, economic, and political questions."

While these deposits do not relate directly to the cities that scientists advocate building off our coasts, the information is one more example of the richness and variety of the resources the sea can yield to humans.

5

Background for Aquaculture

Despite all we are learning about the sea, our relationship to it is still primitive. We have harnessed the resources of the land but largely overlooked the possibilities of the sea.

American farmers each year produce a fabulous yield of grain and meat as a result of a highly developed technology. Yet American fishermen, like those of all countries, are using methods that are in some respects downright ancient. The product of the world's fisheries today is nothing much to brag about. And in light of a world where many millions are always on the verge of starvation while many others actually die of it, our ignoring the opportunities of food in the sea is deplorable.

Square mile for mile, the sea is estimated to be potentially more productive than the land. Yet the present 60 million tons of fish we harvest annually represent only one to two percent of the food consumed each year by the peoples of the world.

Other than cultivating the seabed on a small scale for oysters and lobsters, humans have not bothered to fertilize the spawning grounds of fish. For some 7,000 years man has been raising plants and animals on land. From the earliest days he understood that the growing of crops required preparation of the soil, irrigating it, and proper fertilizing. Proper harvesting has always involved putting something back into the soil—otherwise, the soil would not yield.

51

We learned that the same approach is necessary to sustain a steady supply of game food. But we did not learn it until the 1800s. By the turn of the century millions of bison had vanished from the American prairies. In the eastern part of the country the white-tailed deer population had dwindled to less than one million. Today game is abundant again in North America. The white-tailed deer population has reached 15 million. The buffalo, or bison, is raised commercially; a herd of some two dozen around 1900 has grown to 50,000 animals today. The reason: we learned the meaning of conservation. We introduced sensible hunting regulations, established game preserves, and protected the game.

Now we must do the same to benefit from the ocean's vast food supplies. They must be harvested properly. Spawning grounds for fish may be developed through fertilizing, and other types of "gardening" on the ocean floor may flourish with the use of proper techniques. When humans begin to develop the new age of aquaculture, it will involve, among many things, following strict rules and regulations so that certain species of fish will not be wiped out. It will involve antipollution measures, vast scientific research programs employing numerous marine biologists, new and sophisticated fishing methods, and efficient processing plants. Above all, the development of aquaculture as a fundamental "way of life" can be greatly aided by the cities in the sea of the future.

Fish will become *the* most important of human foodstuffs. Subsidiary uses of fish and fish products already include the manufacture of nitrogenous fertilizer from fish and fish scraps and the extraction of fish liver oils as one of the sources of vitamin D. Fish scales are sometimes used in the making of artificial pearls. Isinglass, a form of gelatin, is prepared from the bladders of certain species of fish, and glue is made from fish offal. Other subsidiary products no doubt will be developed.

Approximately 30,000 species of fish are known, which is considerably more than the number of any other class of vertebrates. Fish are widely distributed all over the world and are found wherever there is water. By far the greatest number of species of oceanic fish is found in tropical waters, and the majority of tropical species live in the Indian

Author Erik Bergaust during a visit to Scripps Institution of Oceanography with the famous research ship "Flip" in the background. (Photo Guido Cassetta)

Ocean and the southwest Pacific. The fish of the northern and southern temperate zones are, in the main, of different genera, but certain genera, such as the hake and the sardine, are found in both zones. The fish of the Arctic and Antarctic belong to different genera entirely.

Tuna, cod, haddock, halibut, flounder—down to the tiny sardine—represent only a few of the oceanic species used for food. Yet these are among the species that will be harvested in increasing numbers in the future. Also, people will increase the "production" of crabs, lobsters, crayfish, clams, and oysters as the aquaculture programs get into high gear.

Some feeble attempts at aquaculture have been undertaken. For example, people have built structures to help salmon reach their spawning grounds. Such salmon nurseries are common in Norway and Canada. Along some coasts oyster growers set out beds of oysters and protective fencing. In the Philippines, Indonesia, Japan, and China people already grow fish and prawns in freshwater ponds. But for the future world population, man will have to start large-scale farming of the sea as he has done for so many thousands of years on land.

Marine biologists, oceanographers, and other scientists are trying to find the best methods for harvesting the ocean's riches. New research results are announced frequently. Already it has been established that aquaculture on a profitable scale will be most beneficial when conducted as part of a sea city complex. The basic reason is that the living organisms in the sea flourish exceptionally well around man-made structures, such as oil rigs, bridge pylons, buoys, and the like. Secondly, it is easier to supervise, control, and harvest the seabed directly from a sea city complex.

The food cycle in the ocean begins with tiny plants and animals floating at or near the surface of the water, depending almost entirely on water currents for their transportation. They are known collectively as plankton and they are well known to man for the discoloration of the water they sometimes cause. They may at times color large areas of the ocean green, red, or many colors in between.

Plankton range in size from microscopic bacteria to forms as large as jellyfish and carry colored granules (most frequently red) in their bodies. These colored organisms are distributed throughout the world from the polar waters to the tropics. Although they occur in almost all waters in large numbers, their color does not become noticeable until they exceed their normal abundance. Millions of organisms in a small volume of water are required for definite discoloration.

When the necessary combination of factors is just right, the plankton reproduces at a great rate and the tremendously increased population is called a "bloom." If these organisms contain pigments, the bloom is visible as discoloration. Some of the factors causing such developments are increased food material, more favorable temperature, and salinity.

The bloom, however, is usually short-lived. This tremendous population begins to compete with itself for food, which is quickly being consumed. Also, the waste products which may have been caused by killing off enemy forms now begin to pollute the water to the point where it kills off the bloom itself. The original situation which made conditions right may now have changed—the temperature may have dropped or risen to an unfavorable point; oxygen may have become scarce; and a change in wind or tide may often be sufficient to dispel the bloom.

As is the case with all living forms, the basic foods for plankton are nutrient chemicals (nitrates, phosphates, dissolved organic matter, and the like), besides the energy from the sun. The plan plankton makes use of these, and the animal plankton lives on the plants.

Coastal waters provide these nutrients in greater abundance than do the open seas because decomposing matter which supplies these chemicals settles to the bottom. In the shallow coastal waters they remain within reach of the plankton near the surface. Also, the population of these waters is greater than that of the open sea, accounting for the large supplies of decomposing material. Organic material washed from the land is another important source of food for the life of the coastal waters.

Life in the sea actually begins with the plankton. If man can control the abundance and the flow of plankton, he will be well on the way to true gardening of seafood. A system for such an accomplishment will have to start with erection of underwater structures or the use of existing steel girders and pylons from sea city construction. When a marine platform, rig, or bridge is constructed, the steel trusses and chains will provide living space on a first-come, first-served basis for the plankton creatures that need a surface on which to grow. At first the pilings will support algae. Then barnacles, anemones, and other suspension feeders will affix themselves to the rig. These early arrivals attract small fish which nibble on the algae and crustaceans. In turn, small fish lure the larger carnivorous fish. The step-by-step process continues until the biological community has a full representation of feeding types clinging to and living among the sea city's steel supports. Beneath the waves the sea city will consist of a beautiful aquarium. It will be a balanced community of plants and animals.

To sustain this seafood nursery, the marine biologists at a sea city will seek to employ various techniques and methods for controlling pollution, the temperature in the water flowing underneath the city, the salinity, fertilization, and even aerating of the seafood garden from perforated pipes on the bottom which carry air. This latter system may be useful to stimulate the flow of nutrients to those areas most conveniently accessible for the sea farming. We can induce upwellings of mineral-rich cold water through long tubes to the deep-sea layers. The rising bubbles of air would carry nutrients up with them.

Such a system may be deployed on a large scale for stimulating nutrients to a vast fishing area. It might even be possible to cause an upwelling in the Gulf Stream, for example, by anchoring a quantity of submerged buoys across the Straits of Florida with huge "otter boards" attached to them deep in the water. Each of these boards, which look like rudder-type planes, would be tilted in such a way as to deflect the cold bottom waters upward. This system would fetch nutrient minerals up to the top, turn the Gulf Stream off the southeastern United States green with blooming plankton, and conceivably boom the fishing industry in the south Atlantic states.

Submersibles like this for support of tomorrow's aquaculture centers may be very complex and fitted with as much sophisticated equipment and instrumentation as a space capsule. (U.S. Navy)

Sea farming at a sea city site might actually require people to go underwater in order to do the job right. They would use specially designed seafloor tractors and other equipment, including submersible robot-type vessels, for plowing and weeding as well as for maintenance of buoy systems and nutrient pipelines.

Sir Alister Hardy of Oxford University believes that a first step in sea city farming will involve making a distinction between creatures humans can eat and those they cannot. The latter will have to be classified as weeds and rooted out. As long ago as World War I a marine biologist calculated that weeds—that is, inedible creatures like brittle stars and starfish—devour all but a tiny percentage of the fish food available in the sea.

To clear away these weeds so that the fish can get at least twenty percent of the available food, Professor Hardy expects that sea farmers "working in two-hour shifts from a mother ship above . . . will be driving pressure-proof submarine tractors down below." Equipped with buoyancy tanks and driven by propellers, these submarine tractors will be able to skim the bottom in the growing season, raking off the starfish and other weeds. Later, when harvest time comes, the same tractors with their deep-sea drivers at the helm will whisk nets through the same area and collect the fish that have grown fat on their unshared sea-bottom fare.

Eventually marine biologists working at cities in the sea will learn to find the proper methods and techniques for raising specific species of fish. Thus, while the sea farm at one sea city might specialize in raising bluefish and rockfish, another establishment might concentrate on fish of the flounder family. A highly sophisticated method of plankton fertilization and temperature control—plus use of chemical nutrients and "additives"—may make this possible sometime in the future.

Experts agree that the United States' requirements for seafood are expected to double in the next two decades. Improving current fishing methods will only help a bit in coping with the situation. Old-fashioned methods are becoming too costly; a full-fledged sea farming program is the only long-term solution. In Asia, Africa, and Latin America, where birthrates are soaring, survival may hinge on the development of underwater farming.

6

Engineering the Sea Farm

Sea city farming will do away with many conventional methods and equipment. A vast fleet of trawlers and other vessels may not be needed. New methods employing floating rigs with sophisticated net systems for scooping up the fish, as well as pipeline slurries using vacuum suction, will be introduced. There will be much activity on the ocean floor, and many scientists are already at work designing prototype equipment which will be required to sustain the sea farms of the future.

The "Deep Quest" is such a piece of equipment. It is one of many submersible vessels which can be sent down to depths of 4,000 feet to "map" the ocean floor. The geotechnical surveying of the ocean floor will tell scientists how to go about developing a sea farm, what kind of structures will be required, the potential for plankton growth in the area, temperatures, salinity, and currents.

Structures which form the foundation of a city in the sea will become artificial reefs. Ever since the oil industry went to sea and offshore drilling got under way, this has been a known fact to fishermen. The teeming life beneath the waves around the oil rigs in the Gulf of Mexico is no secret: the rigs are where the biggest fish are caught. Marine biologists have observed reef communities as they develop predictably on every new rig from a few simple life forms at first to complex ecological systems. The oil rig reef community is as delicate and varied as a tropical coral reef. The same situation pertains to bridge pylons up and down hundreds of American waterways. For example, the best fishing spots in the entire Chesapeake Bay are found underneath the huge spans and among the pylons of the twin Chesapeake bridges.

Artificial structures for sea cities, bridges, oil rigs, and runways cannot be seen from land or from above the surface. They will not clutter the landscape and spoil the environment. Yet some may wonder if all that steel and concrete will cause pollution on the ocean floor and spoil aquatic life. As we have seen, however, this is not the case. On the contrary, man-made underwater structures mean a boom for aquatic life and a subsequent potential of great magnitude for wiping out the food crisis for mankind.

Successful aquaculture in the future must be conducted on the basis of a wise and fine balance between many types of engineering and technology. A manufacturing plant or sewage facility at a sea city cannot dump hot water back into the ocean at random. After the completion of a cooling cycle, the heated water must be channeled through a grid of submerged pipes before it can be discharged into the sea. Temperature variations affect aquatic life to a great extent. A few degrees up or down the thermometer scale may mean certain death to the organisms in the sea.

In addition to elaborate temperature control facilities, farmers at the sea city must have facilities for controlling the salinity of the water that flows over and around the fish nurseries. Among the hazards that fish and shellfish must survive if they are to grow old enough to be harvested is too much fresh water.

Lobster, crab, and shrimp are specialties which may be farmed extensively because they are highly prized as particularly delicious food. Also, oysters, crabs, clams, and mussels will constitute a practical and profitable crop for the aquaculturalist in the future because they are fairly stationary on the sea floor and easy to raise. But having the right amount of fresh and/or salt water at the right time will be a major factor in the size of the crop obtainable by commercial fisheries. Marine biologists have established, for example, that adult oysters cannot

In preparing for tomorrow's aquaculture, scientists send to the bottom special cameras for photographing the sea floor to determine if it is suitable for sea farming. (U.S. Information Service)

feed properly when salinity drops below about five parts per thousand. Furthermore, oysters cannot reproduce in fresh water.

The blue crab, the basis for a large commercial fishing industry in the Chesapeake Bay, is apt to grow to enormous proportions when farming at sea cities in the area gets under way. Eighty million pounds of blue crabs valued at approximately six million dollars are already taken during an average ten-year period in the area. However, the salinity requirements of this crab clearly point to the need for careful salination control.

The blue crab mates in the middle and upper portions of the Chesapeake Bay and in rivers of low to moderate salinity. Sex ratios in commercial catches vary according to how salty the water is. After mating, females migrate to saline areas because their eggs hatch prematurely (and the larval crabs die) if salinity is too low. Males do not need to journey to areas of higher salinity and remain in brackish water, where they spend the winter in the bottom. In nearly fresh water the catch is almost one hundred percent male. Near the ocean it is almost all female. Newly hatched crabs start to move up the bay, and the young crabs hatched during the fall reach the upper bay in April or May.

At a certain stage in their development, clams, mussels, and oysters are sedentary, which makes them victims of the water in which they exist. If the water does not contain a certain percentage of salt, these mollusks will not survive.

Certain marine finfish also have varying saline requirements for different stages in their life cycles. For example, the striped bass female will not spawn until she reaches fresh, or virtually fresh, water, and she needs spawning areas with a lot of moving water. The young then move to the more saline tidal creeks, where they feed in the marshes.

Salinity is involved in the complex of biological, chemical, and hydrological factors contributing to the "red tide" outbreaks along the coastal waters of North America. Red tides are, as mentioned earlier, the blooms of plankton organisms which may or may not cause a red discoloration of the water, and may or may not be lethal to fish and other aquatic organisms.

Waters of different salinities have different densities, and when they come together it is possible for a mass or patch of lower density and salinity than the normal water to form. If this mass satisfies the nutritional and other requirements of the plankton, a temporary bloom can result. If a red tide produces toxins, the paralytic poison becomes concentrated in such bivalves as clams and mussels. Since scallops and oysters often live in deeper waters, they are less frequently infected. Lobsters, shrimp, crabs and deep-sea fish are not usually affected because they are not "filter feeders."

Filter feeders take seawater into their bodies and screen out microscopic organisms as the water passes through them. If the plankton organisms produce toxins, these can build up within the mollusks which feed on them. If these, in turn, are eaten by humans, the toxins can cause paralysis.

At the present time there is nothing used chemically or physically to stop the red tide. However, this problem is of such magnitude that it will require perfect control at the sea farms and cities in the sea of the future. Any control agent would have to be selective; that is it must kill the toxin-producing organism without harming other species. The usual cure has been to wait for cooler water and weather, which seems to cause a reversal and a dispersal of the concentrations.

Once this happens, the clams and other mollusks, which apparently suffer no ill effects from the organisms within them, can pass off the accumulated toxins. As they feed, they dilute the toxins until they themselves are harmless.

In addition to natural phenomena which are unpredictable, shellfish have to endure some of man's activities which alter salinity levels. Many estuaries are becoming much fresher, and, as a result, formerly productive oyster beds are in danger. The causes are still being researched, but the changes may be due to increasing urbanization along the upper estuaries, resulting in increased runoff of water from developed lands through storm sewers.

Diluting the salt level is not the only danger to fish and shellfish. They face the same danger from the reverse—the intrusion of a salt wedge from the ocean or bay farther upstream than is usual. Any change in the flow regime of a river which alters its estuary pattern may greatly decrease fisheries because a critical mix of fresh and saltwater is often necessary for spawning. It is evident that while we cannot always control natural phenomena which alter salinity in bays and estuaries, it becomes a most important thing for the aquaculturalists of tomorrow to regulate the flow of water from the land, abide by stringent anti-pollution laws, and employ equipment to manipulate the flow of fresh water and/or salt to the seabed farm areas. Obviously a large-scale aquaculture operation will require much caretaking, introduction of sophisticated pumping, desalting, and filtering equipment, and efficient control of nutrient and plankton flow.

All aquaculture activity in the future will be regulated and must follow rules and regulations pertaining to endangered species. Fish catches of some species will be restricted upward to a given maximum for any sea farm or aquaculture center. Such quota systems will differ from one area to another and must be supervised and policed by the authorities.

Not until recently, when man learned to understand the salmon's life cycle, did we bother to take the necessary steps to protect this valuable fish by introducing strict quota systems and conservation programs. The sturgeon is another fish which man is working desperately to bring back to a state of abundance.

The fact that the United States will double its seafood harvest in the next two decades indicates that a great expansion in seafood processing facilities is in the offing. Existing processing plants, canning factories, and shipping terminals are located in congested areas along the coasts. It is difficult for most of these plants to expand. There just isn't enough land or space available for them to do so. Furthermore, with the coming of the cities in the sea, it would be logical and profitable for them to build new facilities out at sea, next to the sea farms. Also, locating them in such areas will make it considerably more convenient for the fishing fleet which operates far out in the ocean to unload its catches quickly.

Seafood is marketed in either fresh, frozen, or canned form. With sea farming adjacent to the cities in the sea, which will be linked to the mainland by tunnels, bridges, or other pier structures and pipelines, more fresh fish can be marketed in the future. The product may be slurried in ice water to a shipping terminal and brought to market much faster, or it may be packed in ice-filled crates at the sea city and hauled away to receiving ports up and down the coast by small freighters, some of them of the refrigeration type.

Processing plants for cleaning, packing, and freezing seafood most certainly will be built "next door" to the sea farms. The same applies to canning factories. A subsequent development will be the need for warehouse and refrigerated "locker plant" facilities and on-the-site harbors for bigger freighters to haul away these seafood products.

One can only speculate about how many people a future city in the sea will employ. It seems clear that the activities connected with sea farming and the handling of seafood products alone will require hundreds, if not thousands, of workers. There will be administration people who will supervise the overall operation, as well as maintenance experts to carry out the routine functions that keep the man-made island going. And there will be engineers and technicians who monitor the systems needed to control the flow of nutrients and plankton, salt and/or fresh water, and who keep track of pollution. Laboratory technicians will be responsible for monitoring environmental control, checking bacteria contents, and so on. Other people will be employed by the authorities who must oversee health control and catch regulations. Obviously, there must be a weather station connected with the project, as well as a coast-guard rescue station.

Then there are the "underwater fishermen"—the farmers who will work on the bottom, manipulating the fertilizing and weeding with submersibles and the seafloor tractors. (A submersible is any vehicle that can be maneuvered under water.) Up above, other fishermen will operate the barges, floating rigs, nets and seines, and other gear for catching the fish or scooping up the oysters, clams, and crabs. Other experts will man the piers and the docks for unloading and shipping; and

67

An aquanaut examines giant California kelp being grown off San Clemente Island in the Ocean Food and Energy Farm Project. The project is managed by the Naval Undersea Center in San Diego. (U.S. Navy)

there will be crane operators, truck drivers, and warehousemen, as well as the crews of the small and large freighters. In the locker plants the refrigeration experts will operate, and in the canning factories and processing plants scores of women and men will be busy readying the seafood products for marketing or storage. Also, there must be a health service or clinic available, as well as food dispensaries for workers.

Remember that these workers are affiliated only with the aquaculture aspect of the sea city. Imagine how many more people from all walks of life will be involved if such a city consists of a complex made up of such things as a port for supertankers, an airport, a sewage plant, a desalination plant, and an electric power station.

It is difficult to state what particular aspect of tomorrow's sea cities is most important. In a time of energy crisis sources of power are vital. Yet to society in general it is equally important that desalination plants be built to provide much-needed fresh water; that sewage plants be constructed to cope with increased population; that airports be built without destruction of thousands of acres of prime land; and that power plants be moved away from metropolitan areas.

If, on the other hand, it develops that a shortage of food is the overriding problem of the world, then aqualculture will be the most important aspect of the cities in the sea.

As agriculture involves both the production of plant crops and raising of livestock, so aquaculture involves plants as well as fish.

Today the Japanese are in the van as aquaculturalists. For generations they have raised in brackish waters along their coasts an alga called nori, of which they are especially fond. At present they raise an annual crop of nori valued at $25 million. It is popular as a vegetable rich in vitamin A. When the stalks and fronds are dried and pressed, they can be ground up and the powder is mixed with water to make a soft drink. The Japanese use nori in making soup and sandwiches; they also mix it with meats, or coat it with sugar and eat it as candy.

But the most widely used water plant along many shores of the Pacific is kelp. The wide, brownish-green kelp fronds, usually growing in cold water on rocky coasts, may reach a length of 100 feet, and one plant alone may weigh 200 pounds. In some shore areas of the Pacific, where kelp-raising has become an important business, the plants are harvested by craft which look like huge seagoing lawn mowers. These may gather hundreds of tons a day. They cut off only the top four or five feet of the fronds in order to conserve the crop and let sunlight penetrate to younger shoots.

When kelp is harvested without restriction, the entire crop is destroyed. In California, where the kelp industry is important, harvesting is carefully controlled. Plots of twenty-five square miles of water are leased to farmers, whose harvesting work is strictly enforced.

Kelp has many purposes. It is eaten fresh as a vegetable, used as fodder for livestock, and as fertilizer for root plants. Kelp is the principal source of a remarkable product called algin, whose uses are endless. It is an important ingredient in the making of drugs, antibiotics, and surgical threads. Algin is used in ice cream, chocolate milk, frozen foods, puddings, cheeses, plastics, polishes, tires, etc. The list goes on and on. And scientists emphasize that it has great potential as a source of methane and other fuels.

In an effort to explore and develop the capacity to raise the giant California kelp and other marine plants, private industry and agencies of the federal government have collaborated in what is called the Ocean Food and Energy Farm Project. Its findings could have great impact on the aquacultural activities of future cities in the sea. The project, managed by the Naval Undersea Center in San Diego, hopes to complete development of a 100,000-acre farm system on the Atlantic or Pacific coast some time between 1985 and 1990.

Dr. Howard A. Wilcox, the project manager based in San Diego, recently discussed the concept of an experimental marine farm project such as that started off the northern tip of San Clemente Island, off the California coast. The water surrounding the crop is to be "fertilized" and temperature-conditioned by bringing up cool, nutrient-rich waters from a depth of 1,000 feet or so. Additional nutrients can be supplied from the farm's processing plants. One idea calls for a metal mesh to

The Work Systems Package, used in undersea harvesting of marine plants, is shown here mounted to the Naval Undersea Center's unmanned submersible CURV III, which transported it to the work site off San Clemente. (U.S. Navy)

be placed 40 to 80 feet below the ocean surface, with holdfasts of the plants attached to the mesh at intervals. Another idea being evaluated would have the plants drift freely in clumps on the surface without underwater supports.

The findings of the Ocean Food and Energy Farm Project will eventually be of great significance when we start to colonize the sea with city complexes.

7

Toward the Age of Fusion Power

Four billion tons of sediment are washed into streams annually as a result of land misuse; 1,687,825 acres of wildlife habitat have been destroyed by surface mining. In seven states alone, more than 17 million acres of wetlands have been destroyed. (They are Arkansas, California, Florida, Illinois, Indiana, Iowa, and Missouri; and the lost acreage represents 45.7 percent of all the wetlands in these states.)

Logging operations leave 25 million tons of debris in the forests every year; approximately one million acres of forests are clear-cut annually. Right-of-way for 300,000 miles of overhead power lines requires four million acres. Four billion tons of raw materials are consumed annually in U.S. production, most of which are eventually disposed of as waste on the land.

Population and market demands between now and the year 2000 will call for the duplication of all that has been built in the history of the United States—a new school for an old one, new pipelines for old, and so on; airports, highways, housing, shopping centers, office buildings, and factories.

Urban sprawl may eat up 19.7 million more acres by the year 2000. That is an area equivalent to the states of New Hampshire, Vermont, Massachusetts, and Rhode Island. Another 3.5 million acres may be paved over for highways and airports. Seven million acres may pass over from agricultural use to recreation and wildlife areas. Another five million may be lost to agriculture for public facilities, second-home development, and waste-control projects.

Between now and 1990 as many as 492 power stations may be built, many of them needing cooling ponds of 2,000 acres or more. Also by 1990 another two million acres of right-of-way may be required for 200,000 additional miles of power lines. At stake, really, are the nation's irreplaceable estuaries, wetlands, beaches, flood plains, swamps, river- and lakefronts, farms, forests, and scenic uplands. Contrary to the prevailing view, land spoilation is an infinitely more critical threat to the environment than air and water pollution.

These facts and figures developed by the Environmental Protection Agency clearly show how imperative it is that we use the space the sea offers. It is equally clear that the need for power, both electric and fuel, will always be with us in our booming society. To put the power stations offshore will probably become the rule, rather than the exception. Already there are many major industries involved in the design of offshore power plants because the electric utility industry knows it must meet the demands of our growing society on a steadily rising scale. But it must meet these demands in a manner consistent with preservation of the environment at the same time that it overcomes present problems of fossil fuel shortages and power plant siting, licensing, construction, and financing.

The concept of the floating nuclear power plant attempts to reduce the problems associated with these requirements for utilities having coastal territory or interconnections with coastal utilities. The proposal for such power plants involved a nuclear generating station of standardized design constructed on a floating platform in a shipyardlike manufacturing facility. Both plant and platform will utilize existing, proven technology. Plant components and systems are nearly identical to those which have been built on land so far. The supporting platform draws on the best knowledge and experience of marine safety and engineering. As this book went to press, some of these plants were under construction in Jacksonville, Florida, in a specialized facility with some

14,000 people employed. The completed and tested plants will be towed from Jacksonville to the utility sites and permanently moored in a protective breakwater. Underwater cables will transmit the power from a substation on a platform to a switchyard on the shore for distribution to coastal load centers. The concept permits plant siting in many locations from very near the shore to up to several miles offshore, depending upon water depth and other site considerations.

One typical plant will provide 1,150 megawatts of energy. It measures approximately 400 square feet in plan and extends about 180 feet above the waterline. It will draw about 30 feet of water and displace approximately 150,000 tons, and it will have a watertight deck at its 40-foot level.

The heat sink for the main condensers is provided by circulating seawater to the tune of 900,000 gallons per minute from inside the breakwater. This water is passed through the condensers and returned to the ocean outside the breakwater. The floating design is such that the plant operation and maintenance will be essentially identical to that of a comparably sized land-based plant. Depending upon the operating philosophy of the project and the particular site location and conditions, the actual crew kept on board the platform plant will vary. Routine and periodic maintenance can be performed by additional personnel brought to the plant as required.

A breakwater will be designed and constructed, then the plant will be installed in it. Further steps will be designing and constructing the mooring system for the plant, the power cable from the plant to the shore-based transmission system, the circulating water discharge system, and any shore-based servicing facilities. The breakwater is designed to prevent damage to the plant by ship collision and wave motion. It will be founded on the seabed and will extend well above sea level to prevent excessive loading and wave action on the plant by the worst possible storms and hurricanes. The breakwater consists of a concrete caisson core approximately 80 feet in width, with a rock/rubble mound and armor layer facing and topping the caisson.

Caissons will be constructed at a concrete casting yard and towed

75

to the site where they will be lowered to the ocean bottom, after being filled with sand. The rock portion of the core of the breakwater will then be put in place by bottom-dump barges. The bottom layer will be of sand and gravel; the intermediate layer of larger-sized stones. The outer layer of material will be an armor layer in the form of large multi-ton precast concrete structures called dolosses.

The mooring system will be designed to accommodate the vertical motion of the plant under normal and storm tide conditions, but will prevent excessive horizontal movement, even under the most severe storm conditions.

The impact of the offshore installation on the environment has been reviewed and evaluated by many experts on the same basis as a comparable land-based installation. They have established that certain features and characteristics of the offshore plant offer ways to further minimize the impact of electric power plants on the environment. The offshore installation will have favorable implications for land utilization. Two offshore units in a common breakwater will occupy only 70 to 90 acres of ocean bottom, plus a small shoreland site area for docking and support facilities. This can be contrasted with the approximately 500 acres required for equivalent land-based units. Except for the minor intrusion of the shore base, an offshore nuclear plant will not change the uses of the adjacent coastline and waters.

The breakwater and plant-circulating water intake system can also be designed to minimize the impact on the local marine life. Intake openings are about 2,000 square feet in total area, providing an intake velocity of one foot per second. In addition, the intake screens are flush with the platform, and the breakwater will serve as a breeding ground for marine life, as described previously.

Before long, two nuclear power plants will go into operation off the shores of New Jersey. Owned by the Public Service Gas & Electric Company, they will provide much-needed additional electric power for the state. The design parameters for the New Jersey facilities call for the nuclear power plant to occupy the center portion of a huge platform with the containment structure and refueling building its most distinguishing features. The pressurized water reactor nuclear steam supply system is a standard Westinghouse four-loop unit with ice condenser containment.

The instrumentation and control systems are consistent with modern power plant practice and include centralized control rooms and local control stations. These systems enable plant operating personnel to effectively monitor and safely operate the plant. Administration and service facilities provide working and living space for operating, administrative, and maintenance personnel, and supplies for normal and emergency conditions. Specific facilities include a cafeteria, bedrooms, administrative offices, maintenance supply rooms, and recreation rooms. The facilities and arrangement assumes that the plant is staffed on a three-day, two-shift basis, with two shifts transported to the plant every three days, either by ship or helicopter.

The platform serves as the foundation of the plant. It consists of a 40-foot deep grillage arrangement of sheer webs separating the bottom shell (0-foot level) and the strength deck at the 40-foot level. The strength deck and the bottom shell are strengthened by longitudinal stiffeners and transverse girders. The platform's all-welded, carbon-steel plate-stiffener framing is designed to meet the most stringent requirements.

Provisions are made for supplying potable water, for collecting and treating crew-generated waste, and for removing excess water from bilges of watertight compartments and exposed weather surfaces. The man-made islands are also designed with a low silhouette; when viewed from three miles, the offshore installation appears similar to a large ship passing by.

The siting criteria for any offshore installation must necessarily be very strict, particularly so for a nuclear power plant. They are just as stringent as for land-based nuclear plants. In fact, an almost unbelievable amount of research and scientific studies must be accomplished before any offshore facility can be planned and its site selected. Seismic and geologic history, local geology and seismology, faults, maximum earthquake accelerations, ground strength, soil composition, and related investigations must be made. The purpose is to confirm the suitability of a given site to support the breakwater and the plants for more than forty years, without danger of exceeding the design limits of those structures and equipment.

Nuclear power plants will not dump any radioactive wastes into the ocean. Such material will be packaged in sealed containers, as is the case with land-based nuclear plants, and transported to government agencies for proper handling and disposal. People still talk about the "danger" connected with radioactive fallout from nuclear plants. But no such accidents have happened. Furthermore, our technology and know-how have reached a level where the operation of nuclear plants has become just as safe as the operation of conventional plants. Even so, it is likely that the floating nuclear power plants will be isolated from other sea structures and facilities for many years to come.

However, in the distant future such plants probably will become part of a multipurpose sea city. The breakwaters needed for the power plants also may be built to serve other installations, such as sewage plants, canning factories, airports, and sea farms. Breakwaters are particularly suited as foundations for runways, for example.

The principle of floating platforms is a logical one for power plants, as well as for superports and several other facilities. Thus it is likely that tomorrow's cities in the sea will be designed as complexes using *both* the floating platform technique and systems having structures anchored to the bottom. In the distant future it is also possible that many additional purposes will be found for the sea cities. Someday we may actually find out that it will be less expensive to build plants and office buildings and other structures in the sea. The cost of downtown land on the mainland will have skyrocketed to such fantastic levels that it may be cheaper to rent space in the ocean!

Well into the twenty-first century our scientists are expected to provide us with yet another spectacular development—the introduction of *fusion* power.

The nuclear power manufactured today is derived from *fission,* i.e., splitting, of atoms. A fast-moving subatomic neutron splits the nucleus of an atom of uranium fuel, for example. Both fragments fly apart and create heat by colliding with other atoms of the fuel. Meanwhile, other neutrons are ejected from the fissioned uranium nucleus to split additional uranium nuclei, thus producing more heat and freeing more neutrons to split more nuclei, and so forth, in a continuing chain reaction.

Fusion, on the other hand, is based on the *merging* of particles. When nuclei of hydrogen, for example, are made to merge under the impact of a collision caused by heating the gas containing them, they will become fused and will form a new unstable nucleus that must give off either one proton or one neutron. This releases tremendous energy. Actually, the hydrogen bomb is based on this principle. So is the power process in the sun.

Though fusion power has been produced in laboratories for a split second, it is still a long way from becoming a practical reality. In the meantime, we are obliged to press on with our known resources and energy-producing elements—the fossil fuels, oil and gas, and "common" nuclear power from uranium fission reactors.

8

A New Breed of Divers

As people begin to colonize the sea, they will use many different types of tools and equipment to carry out a number of functions on the ocean floor. Some operations will be done automatically by mechanical robots, remote-controlled vehicles, buoys, and the like. But in most cases people themselves will be directly involved. They will operate either as divers or by using various types of submersible vessels.

Increased activity on the ocean floor will require specialist divers by the thousands. It is a career for both young men and women to consider seriously. Many new and advanced types of equipment will be developed to make it possible for the divers to perform and accomplish various tasks.

In order to function properly modern divers must have special suits, helmets, goggles, air supply, and other means for operating under water. So-called skin divers and scuba divers, carrying their air supply in tanks strapped to their backs, will always be limited as to how far they may roam from their "mother ship" above, or how deep they may go without being crushed by excessive pressures.

In measuring water depth one *atmosphere* is equal to 33 feet beneath the surface. The pressure measurement for the first atmosphere is computed by adding 14.7 pounds per square inch (atmospheric pressure at sea level) to the pressure measurement per foot of depth in the first atmosphere of water. In other words, the weight of the air at sea level must be added to the weight of the first 33 feet of water in order to give an accurate measurement of pressure at any further depth.

The deeper we travel under water, the greater the pressure becomes, as the molecules are squeezed more closely together. It is usually possible to dive in the first atmosphere without equipment and without pressure problems. Beyond this depth pressure becomes important as a factor affecting the functions of the human body. Skin divers safely dive in this range without compressed air tanks and with face masks only.

In the next six atmospheres the need for diving suits and compressed air tanks (scuba equipment) becomes urgent for dives of any duration. The safe range for scuba equipment is up to six atmospheres, or 198 feet. The extreme pressures at lower depths make diving with scuba equipment impractical and unsafe, because the mixture of gases (oxygen, helium, and carbon dioxide) fed from the diving equipment must be controlled carefully to safeguard the life of the diver. Deep-sea diving equipment is usually used at these depths, and the air supply is fed to the diver from the surface through his hose. A helium-oxygen mixture, rather than a nitrogen-oxygen mixture, is usually used at depths of more than 200 feet.

In scuba diving the tanks (cylinders) used are filled with compressed air, not just pure oxygen. The greater the depth of the dive, the more compressed air the diver will require, and it is important in diving to consider the amount of air each cylinder will deliver at different depth levels. When a diver plans a dive of 200 feet, it is necessary to know how long the air will last at this depth.

The greater the pressure and depth, the faster the air will be consumed by the diver. This phenomenon becomes important when divers may have to rise too quickly to the surface because of an emergency. Pressure decreases on the way up, and and too much air absorbed too quickly in the lungs expands them to the point where they might easily burst. The air molecules become more widely spaced as the pressure of deep depths ceases to "squeeze" the lungs. Many deaths have occurred in diving because of fast returns from great depths.

Diving has become a popular sport. Better diving suits and equipment have made it possible for thousands of people to take up the sport of skin or scuba diving, even in winter cold. Here a Navy frogman serenades the crew of a vessel from his icy stage. (U.S. Navy)

The art of diving involves many other intricacies and dangers. Most are fully understood by scientists, and researchers and engineers are able to work on designs for more advanced equipment. In the next few decades much of this important gear will be improved. Diving will beome less complex and less dangerous. Devices and equipment enabling divers to ascend properly and safely will be introduced, as will materials (most likely synthetic) for construction of more efficient suits.

Also, divers operating at sites involving ocean floor construction, tank farms, and aquaculture centers will have the advantage of working from underwater habitats and stations located on the bottom. This will make it possible to prolong the time of operation. Eventually, it will become possible for divers to "refuel" without interrupting their work or operations. Portable compressed-air tanks may be brought along or stored at a work site. A simple method for changing tanks in the water will be introduced. Thus the day will come when divers will be able to operate without interruption for as long as they can physically cope. A four- to six-hour "workday" may become feasible.

Working in the neighborhood of a habitat or seafloor station will make it possible to carry out a job around the clock, using teams of divers who work in shifts. When one team returns to the habitat for food and rest, another team will replace the first one at the work site. Then a third team moves out; next a fourth team, and so on. The habitat itself will receive replenishments, supplies, and air from a mother ship on the surface, or from a depot-type station connected with a sea city or other installation up above.

Ocean floor habitats will enable divers to work and live below the waves for long periods of time. In this fashion the value of the divers will become increasingly important. In addition to the employment of diver teams, an array of submersible vessels will be developed in the future building of cities in the sea.

Scientists are developing new types of underwater vehicles, instruments, and techniques that will enable man to go deeper than ever before, remain at those depths for longer periods, and travel along the seafloor for greater distances. Amazing advances are expected in these areas within the next few decades.

At the same time new devices are being perfected to rescue men and their vessels if serious trouble occurs. Scientists have also suggested a worldwide network of automatic underwater stations that will continuously record data on deep currents, temperature, salt content, and other conditions on the seafloor. These stations would flash sound beam reports to ship and shore stations. They also plan to use acoustic beacons placed on the bottom to guide ships under way. These will be an improvement over present radio aids now used for navigation since they will be closer together and nearer to ships at sea.

Some forthcoming oceanographic instruments are aimed at helping us learn more about the vital, but still little understood, affect of the sea on weather changes. Thus within the next few decades we will find ourselves the beneficiaries of a worldwide system of radio buoys designed to record and transmit variations in ocean currents, for we now know that currents influence day-to-day weather.

Hurricanes and other storms will someday be tracked with earthquake recorders, or seismometers, left at the bottom of the sea. It has long been suspected that storms at sea transmit disturbances to the ocean floor, where they cause small tremors in the earth's crust. A network of these instruments, connected to shore stations by cable, will make it unnecessary to send planes out in severe weather, as is being done today, to plot storm tracks. Scientific information collected in these ways will be fed to computers along with data obtained from land-based observations and information from a network of space satellites. This comprehensive coverage will make it possible for man to take great strides forward; indeed, someday he may even be able to control the weather.

In the next fifty years much of the automatic buoy equipment will be nuclear-powered, possibly by radioactive isotope reactor, and it will operate for several years without maintenance or "refueling." Some buoys and unmanned beacons will operate electrically, the power being fed to them through ocean floor cables from a central nuclear power plant located somewhere off the coast of the mainland.

However, this equipment, the buoys, beacons, and instrument packages, will need underwater diving and submersible teams to place them on the ocean floor and maintain them in service. Before such networks of automatic equipment are installed along the ocean floor, vast research and mapping must be undertaken by teams of experts. Automatic equipment for mapping the capacity of the ocean floor to handle a variety of "traffic" has already been developed in the United States and is currently being used experimentally in the Pacific. Soon such preliminary work will be common along the coastlines of all the continents.

This research involves a survey of the ocean floor. Charts showing all details, contours, and characteristics of the floor along the continental shelves will someday be available, much as we now have geodetic survey maps of all our land areas. Each map will cover a few square miles of ocean floor area and will be used by engineers and scientists to determine where and how to install automatic equipment.

Within a few decades it may become necessary to regulate, through government controls, the traffic on the ocean floor to prevent accidents of various kinds. Cables, buoys, weather beacons, anchor chains, and other fixed installations will eventually constitute a navigation hazard for divers and submersibles. Some of the equipment may get entangled, power lines may break, oil may be spilled from tank farms or leak from broken pipelines, and submarines may collide with buoys. We can only speculate on the chaos that may develop in ocean science and undersea activity if the question of traffic is not taken seriously. As government-regulated supervision becomes increasingly necessary, it will require the employment of thousands of people.

In the future a governmental "police force" may operate much like the Civil Aeronautics Board and the Federal Aviation Administration, which regulates commercial airplane operations and traffic in the skies.

Surface ships will take part in such operations and permanent floating islands will serve as stations for traffic control. Monitoring will be done with computers, data processing machines, and special underwater electronic communications equipment. Attached to these ships and floating islands will be a fleet of various kinds of submersibles for enforcing the police work and carrying out rescue operations.

Men and women beneath the waves, operating from habitats and as crew members of submersibles, will include laboratory technicians, engineers, scientists, mechanics, repairmen, aquaculturalists, traffic police, and government inspectors. All will have serious and important jobs. Diving for fun will probably not be allowed in areas of heavy industrial and scientific activity near superports, floating power stations, and cities in the sea. Yet more and more underwater "parks" for sports divers will flourish in suitable waters. In the future the aquanaut will be as important as the astronaut.

9

Habitats on the Ocean Floor

At latest count about eighty different submersible vessels are in use in the United States. Many more are under construction. An additional three dozen are in the blueprint stage.

Submersibles fall into two categories: self-propelled submarine vessels designed to travel in the sea for various purposes; and submersible structures designed to rest on the ocean floor and serve as habitats for a crew of several members.

A submersible may be designed for such jobs as the rescue of the crew of a submarine in distress, as an inspection and repair vehicle for transoceanic cables, as an oceanographic research vessel designed to scoop up samples of sediment, and as a salvage vessel designed to assist divers in their efforts to explore sunken wreckage. A habitat, in almost all cases, is designed as an underwater laboratory. It is very similar to a space station in this respect and serves the same purpose. However, while a space station orbits the earth at great speed, an ocean habitat remains in a fixed position.

The original purpose of our space program was to learn if people—astronauts—could live and work in space. In similar fashion, ocean habitats were developed to find out if people—aquanauts—could live and work on the ocean floor. Submersibles and habitats have been developed and built by private industry, scientific organizations, and the U.S. Navy. The Navy is by far the most enthusiastic patron of these underwater programs.

Research and development over many years in the area of submarines and diving bells, coupled with technological breakthroughs in other fields, made it possible for American scientists to make serious advances in the design of modern submersibles in the late 1950s. During the next decade several highly sophisticated vessels were used successfully. Since 1970 some bold projects have gotten under way, some involving habitats with men and women aboard who have remained on the ocean floor for weeks on end.

On February 5, 1969, the habitat Tektite I was lowered off the coast of St. John in the Virgin Islands, where it was fixed on the bottom at 50 feet. Painted white, it was made up of two cylinders, both 18 feet high, 12.5 feet in diameter, and connected with a crawlway tunnel. Each cylinder was two stories high. The lower room of one cylinder contained the living quarters where the crew ate and slept; above that the bridge room packed with laboratory and communications equipment. The lower part of the other cylinder contained the "wet" room that opened into the sea and provided space for storing scuba gear, diving suits, and clothes; above that the fourth room contained the air conditioning, transformer, food freezer, and other equipment.

The habitat was manned by a crew of four scientists using a new technique called saturation diving. This is likely to become widely employed in the future. In this technique the divers, before going down, enter a pressurized tank for a day or two and breathe an atmosphere of hydrogen and oxygen there that is at the same pressure as the habitat below. After the tissues in their bodies become saturated with the gases, they go down. In and around the habitat they are now as much at home as the fish and can stay as long as they want. Decompression is necessary only when they return to the surface.

After sixty days of living on the bottom, the divers left the habitat and returned to the surface. The project proved that men could live and work together in the sea for as long as sixty days without suffering physical, emotional, or mental discomfort or injury; that they could get along with each other under difficult circumstances; and that the saturation diving technique worked. It was a great success for underwater science and for the U.S. Navy.

The Navy then took a big step forward with Tektite II, a habitat designed to remain on the bottom for seven months. Fifty divers and scientists were signed up for the experiment, including five women. The crew operated in teams of five, taking turns remaining below for periods ranging from fourteen to twenty days.

Tektite II was fixed firmly at a depth of 50 feet, while a smaller *minitat* designed to support a crew of two was placed nearby at a depth of 100 feet. The value of the experiment to the Navy, and to the ocean science community, was incalculable. It was the breakthrough engineers and scientists had waited for. It was the proof that space-station-type facilities could be built and successfully inhabited by men for great lengths of time. It also meant that the Navy could encourage industry to proceed with several of the plans which so far had only reached the blueprint stage. Here is what we can expect in the future:

The introduction of self-contained power supply units, such as nuclear isotope reactor packages, will make it possible to build habitats that are completely self-sufficient. In case of foul weather it will be possible to disconnect the umbilical connection to any surface supply ships, temporarily or permanently. If the aquanauts must leave their habitat and ascend to the surface, they will be able to do so without support from the surface. The habitat will be equipped with a "dinghy" submersible or other submarine-type vessel which can take them up and also provide the necessary decompression facilities on board.

As soon as a standard-type habitat unit has been accepted, it will be mass-produced and made as a module which can be used as a building block for an ocean floor complex—a station consisting of numerous habitats interconnected and constructed as a multiple-use laboratory and station for scientists and workers. Within fifty years such ocean floor stations will be common along the continental shelves, providing working space for oceanographers and other scientists, oil pipeline and pumping crews, inspectors, aquaculturalists, and others.

Although basic supplies will be lowered from surface ships at regular intervals, the stations will be able to operate independently for weeks and months at a time, providing its own air supply and pressurization, air conditioning, electrical power for controls and instruments and machinery, and equipped with ample storage facilities for food and other essentials. Fresh water will probably be supplied from separate tanks adjacent to the habitats, and, in case of an emergency, fresh water may be manufactured from distillation of seawater.

Such stations on the ocean floor will be serviced by a crew of 50 to 100 or more people, including cooks, police, firemen, and doctors. The operating force will include mechanics, chemists, data processing experts, laboratory technicians, and scientists.

The purpose of clustering the habitats in multipurpose complexes will be primarily economic. Various endeavors on the ocean floor will logically be placed adjacent to one another. As we have seen, an aquaculture farm will benefit from the steel structures, chains, and buoys of an oil complex because animal life in the sea will flourish around such man-made coral reefs and enhance sea farming. The same floating rigs and pylons on the bottom, which are used to support superports and power plants and even whole cities in the sea, will be constructed for many uses.

Eventually electrical power for the inhabitants of the new sea cities will be supplied through a grid of cables buried under the seafloor from a floating nuclear power plant located inside a breakwater nearby. After a while traffic in and out of the habitat complex will increase to proportions requiring tight navigational control and regulations, as mentioned earlier. Divers may be operating freely as far away from their habitats as 1,500 feet, which was the case in the Tektite program. And submersibles, some of them small and carrying a crew of two, and others operating with a crew of thirty or forty, will come and go.

Someday people will colonize the sea, employing methods we cannot even imagine at present. Impossible? Remember that some of the early European explorers of North America said it would be impossible ever to colonize such a savage land!

Index

The Author

Erik Bergaust has been a space and science writer for more than twenty-five years and is the author of more than forty books. His feature articles for magazines and newspapers have been syndicated throughout the world. He was the first president of the National Space Club in Washington, D.C., is a past president of the National Capital Section of the American Rocket Society, past director of the Aviation & Space Writers Association, and a director of the Environmental Writers Association. He was the founder of *Missiles & Rockets*—first American trade magazine devoted exclusively to rocketry and space flight. Active in the missile and space program as a technical editor of field publications, he has been a special consultant to many aerospace companies. Some of his most recent books from Putnam's include *The Next Fifty Years on the Moon, Rescue in Space,* and *Colonizing the Planets.*